A BUSINESS APPROACH TO ONION FARMING

Complete Entrepreneurial Step By Step Guide To Onion Garden From Scratch

ZHURI HART

DISCLAIMER

This book is intended to provide general information and insights on adopting a business approach to farming. The content within is based on the author's knowledge and experiences up to the date of publication. It is essential to recognize that the field of agriculture is dynamic, influenced by various factors such as market conditions, climate, and regulatory changes.

Readers are advised to conduct thorough research, seek professional advice, and consider their unique circumstances before implementing any strategies or practices discussed in this book. The author and publisher disclaim any responsibility for the accuracy, completeness, or suitability of the information provided. The book is not a substitute for professional advice, and the author and publisher shall not be liable for any damages or losses arising from the use or reliance on the information presented herein.

Individual results may vary, and success in farming enterprises is contingent upon numerous variables. The author encourages readers to consult with relevant experts, agricultural extension services, and legal or financial professionals to tailor strategies to their specific needs and local conditions.

This book is not intended to be a comprehensive guide to all aspects of farming, and readers should exercise their judgment and discretion in applying the principles discussed. The author and publisher do not endorse any specific products, services, or companies mentioned in this book unless explicitly stated.

By reading this book, the reader acknowledges and accepts the inherent uncertainties in agricultural endeavors and agrees to use the information at their own risk.

TABLE OF CONTENTS

ABOUT THE BOOK

"A Business Approach to Onion Farming" is an essential tool for anyone hoping to get into the onion business since it offers a thorough manual that skillfully combines academic understanding with real-world applications. Setting the scene, the introduction provides a thorough overview of the history of the onion growing sector, emphasizes the goals of the book, and specifies who the intended readership is.

The justification for selecting onion farming as the topic is sound, providing insight into the importance of this industry in the agricultural landscape.

The book explores the subtleties of the onion market, analyzing demand dynamics, market trends, and profitability prospects. By doing this, it gives readers a solid understanding of the market dynamics influencing onion agriculture, enabling them to successfully manage the risks and difficulties. To further guarantee that readers have the knowledge and resources they need to make wise decisions, a special section on market research and analysis is included.

The practical side of onion cultivation is discussed in detail. "Getting Started with Onion Farming" offers priceless advice on choosing an area, preparing the soil, and selecting onion varieties. An essential road map for success in the field, the planning and budgeting section walks readers through the complexities of creating a strong business plan, budgeting wisely, projecting finances, and obtaining funding.

An essential component of growing onions well is farming, which is explained in depth. With the knowledge of planting, irrigation, fertilization, controlling pests and diseases, and handling crops after harvest, readers can ensure maximum agricultural productivity.

The addition of a section on technology and equipment highlights the significance of contemporary agricultural methods, stressing automation and efficiency.

Understanding the importance of marketing in a cutthroat agricultural environment, a significant amount of the book is devoted to techniques for advertising onion products. Readers obtain a comprehensive understanding of how to properly position their products in the market, covering everything from branding and packaging to distribution networks, customer relationship building, pricing tactics, and online marketing.

Acknowledging the legal and regulatory terrain, the book discusses environmental rules, agricultural standards compliance, permits, and licensing. This crucial element guarantees that prospective growers of onions not only yield superior crops but also adeptly maneuver through the intricate regulatory landscape.

"A Business Approach to Onion Farming" is essentially a full textbook that provides people with the knowledge and abilities necessary to succeed in the onion farming sector, rather than just a guide.

CHAPTER ONE

ONION FARMING INTRODUCING

COMPREHENDING THE ONION MARKET

With its dynamic and essential role in shaping the agricultural economy worldwide, the onion market is a reflection of regional and global developments that impact its environment. Examining a variety of aspects is necessary to comprehend the onion market's complexities, such as market trends, demand dynamics, profitability potentials, related risks and difficulties, and the crucial function that market research and analysis play.

DEMAND AND MARKET TRENDS

The onion market is prone to constantly changing trends that are shaped by a multitude of factors, including customer tastes, weather patterns, and shifts in the economy. Onion demand has been impacted by a noticeable shift in recent years toward organic and locally produced vegetables. The current market trends have been further impacted by health-conscious consumers and an increasing consciousness of sustainable farming practices. For parties hoping to successfully negotiate the complexity of the onion market, comprehending these changes is essential.

Onions are a staple in many culinary traditions across the globe, and demand for them never goes down. The growing world population and its adaptable application in many cuisines fuel demand. To effectively adjust their tactics and capitalize on particular market niches, market actors must have a thorough awareness of regional variances in consumption patterns.

POSSIBILITY OF FINANCIAL GAIN

Because of its steady demand and vital position in the food business, the onion market offers a significant potential for profitability. Farmers and other industry participants can take advantage of chances for higher yields and improved quality by using the proper agricultural techniques. Furthermore, the market's flexibility to adjust to innovations and technological breakthroughs presents opportunities for increased profitability through cost savings, increased efficiency, and so on.

The complexities of the onion market demand a sophisticated grasp of supply chains, pricing mechanisms, and the influence of geopolitical variables, notwithstanding the sector's inherent profitability. Navigating these complexities is necessary for successful players to realize the market's full potential for profitability.

DANGERS AND OBSTACLES

Risks and difficulties are present in the onion business, ranging from volatile markets to environmental influences. Unseasonal rainfall or extremely high temperatures are two examples of weather-related disturbances that can have a big influence on onion quality and yield.

Furthermore, uncertainties that impact manufacturers and traders might be introduced by changes in trade policies, market volatility, and geopolitical conflicts.

In the onion market, price volatility is a recurring issue that can negatively affect profit margins due to abrupt price changes. Supply and demand must be balanced; otherwise, there may be surpluses or shortages, which could have an impact on prices and profitability.

To effectively reduce these problems, stakeholders must employ risk management measures such as hedging and diversification.

ANALYSIS AND RESEARCH ON THE MARKET

The need for thorough market research and analysis in the quickly changing onion market cannot be emphasized. To make wise judgments, stakeholders must be up to date on global economic trends, emerging technology, and consumer preferences.

Finding possible prospects, analyzing the competition, and comprehending the regulatory environment are all made possible by conducting in-depth market research.

By analyzing market data, such as trade flows, consumption trends, and production statistics, stakeholders are better equipped to make strategic decisions that fit the current dynamics of the market. Moreover, utilizing sophisticated analytics and insights derived from data amplifies the capacity to predict changes in the market and profit from new developments, cultivating a competitive advantage in the onion industry.

The onion market is a complex ecology driven by a variety of factors. To succeed in this industry, stakeholders need to understand the nuances of demand drivers, market trends, profitability potentials, and the risks and difficulties that go along with them.

CHAPTER TWO

BEGINNING THE PROCESS OF ONION FARMING

SELECTING THE IDEAL SITE

Picking a good spot is essential to growing onions successfully. Onions grow best in soil that drains well and receives lots of sunlight. Pick a spot that receives full sun exposure because onions need six hours of sunlight a day at the very least. Make sure there is adequate air circulation in the chosen area as well to ward against the spread of illness.

Steer clear of waterlogged regions since too much moisture can cause onion rot. Since onions are a cool-season crop that thrives in temperatures between 55 and 75 degrees Fahrenheit, take climate and temperature into consideration. To get the best onion growth, examine the soil for pH and nutrient content. A slightly acidic to neutral pH range of 6.0 to 7.0 is the goal.

SOIL QUALITY AND PREPARATION

To supply the nutrients required for growth, one of the most important steps in onion cultivation is soil preparation. Start by removing any rocks, plants, and rubbish from the selected area. Loamy, loose, well-drained soil is ideal for onions. To enhance soil fertility and structure, add organic matter, such as compost or well-rotted manure. Proper root development and easy expansion of onion bulbs are ensured by adequate soil preparation. Raised beds can help with drainage, particularly if the soil in the location you've chosen retains water. Onions can rot in excessively damp conditions, therefore it's important to regularly check the moisture content of the soil and strive for a stable moisture level without becoming swampy.

SELECTION AND VARIETIES OF ONIONS

A good harvest depends on selecting the appropriate onion varieties, taking into account attributes like flavor, size, and storage capacity.

There are three different kinds of onions: short-day, long-day, and intermediate-day. Depending on where you live and how long the days are in your area, choose the right kind. Long-day onions are more suited for northern climates, needing 14–16 hours of daylight, whereas short-day onions are more suitable for southern regions, requiring 10–12 hours. Intermediate-day onions are a versatile crop that may be grown in a variety of environments. Think about your preference for yellow, red, or white onions as well, as each has a distinct flavor.

SEED PURCHASING AND CALIBER

The success of your onion farming endeavor is greatly impacted by the quality of the onion seeds you use. To guarantee that the seeds are of the highest caliber and free of diseases, pick a reliable source. It's advisable to purchase certified onion seeds from trusted sources. The viability and germination rate of the seed are important factors to consider as they have a direct impact on the crop's success.

Check for any signs of disease or damage in the seed before planting. Onion seeds are typically started indoors in seed trays or containers before being transplanted to the final growing location. Adequate care during the seedling stage, including proper watering, temperature control, and exposure to light, will contribute to the development of healthy onion plants ready for transplantation to the field.

CHAPTER THREE

PLANNING AND BUDGETING

CREATING A BUSINESS PLAN

Developing a comprehensive business plan is a foundational step for any entrepreneurial venture, including onion farming. A well-crafted business plan serves as a roadmap, outlining the mission, vision, and goals of the onion farming enterprise.

It should include an analysis of the market, potential competitors, and a detailed description of the farming operations. Additionally, a business plan should delve into the organizational structure, management team, and overall strategy for sustainable growth.

Clear articulation of the value proposition, target market, and marketing strategies are essential components to ensure the success of the onion farming business.

BUDGETING FOR ONION FARMING

Budgeting is a critical aspect of successful onion farming, requiring a meticulous analysis of both fixed and variable costs associated with agricultural operations. The budget should encompass expenses related to land acquisition, seeds, fertilizers, irrigation systems, labor, equipment, and transportation. Accurate budgeting allows for effective resource allocation and risk management. Factors such as seasonal variations, market prices, and unforeseen challenges must be taken into account. Creating a realistic budget helps farmers make informed decisions, optimize resource utilization, and maximize profitability in the dynamic and often unpredictable agricultural sector.

FINANCIAL PROJECTIONS

Financial projections play a crucial role in providing a forward-looking view of the onion farming business. These projections encompass revenue forecasts, expense estimates, and profit margins over a specified period. By analyzing historical data, market trends, and potential risks, farmers can make informed predictions about the financial performance of their onion farming venture. Financial projections aid in assessing the feasibility of the business, attracting potential investors, and setting achievable goals. Regular monitoring and adjustment of financial projections are essential to adapt to changing market conditions and ensure the long-term sustainability of the onion farming enterprise.

SECURING FUNDING AND GRANTS

Securing funding and grants is a pivotal aspect of implementing a successful onion farming operation. Entrepreneurs in agriculture often require financial support for initial investments, operational costs, and expansion plans. Various sources of funding, including government grants, agricultural loans, and private investors, can be explored. The process involves presenting a compelling case for the onion farming project, emphasizing its economic viability, environmental sustainability, and potential impact on local communities. Demonstrating a clear understanding of the market, coupled with a well-structured business plan and financial projections, enhances the likelihood of securing funding and grants to support the growth and development of the onion farming enterprise.

CHAPTER FOUR

FARMING PRACTICES

PLANTING TECHNIQUES

Planting techniques are crucial in determining the success of a crop's growth and yield. Farmers employ various methods to sow seeds and establish crops in their fields. Traditional practices include broadcasting seeds by hand, while modern methods often involve precision planting using specialized equipment. Precision planting allows for optimal spacing between seeds, ensuring efficient use of resources and maximizing yield potential. Additionally, farmers may use techniques such as direct seeding or transplanting, depending on the crop type and environmental conditions.

IRRIGATION METHODS

Irrigation plays a pivotal role in agriculture, especially in regions with irregular rainfall patterns. Farmers employ various irrigation methods to ensure a consistent water supply for their crops. Surface irrigation, such as flood or furrow irrigation, involves flooding the field with water, while drip irrigation delivers water directly to the base of each plant. Sprinkler systems distribute water over crops like natural rainfall. The choice of irrigation method depends on factors such as crop type, soil characteristics, and water availability. Sustainable water management practices are increasingly important to address environmental concerns and optimize resource use.

FERTILIZATION AND SOIL MANAGEMENT

Fertilization and soil management are integral components of modern farming practices aimed at maintaining soil fertility and promoting healthy plant growth. Farmers use fertilizers to supplement essential nutrients in the soil, addressing deficiencies that can limit crop productivity. Sustainable practices include the use of organic fertilizers; cover cropping, and crop rotation to enhance soil structure and nutrient content. Conservation tillage methods help minimize soil erosion and improve water retention. Soil testing is a valuable tool for farmers to assess nutrient levels and make informed decisions regarding fertilization and soil amendments, contributing to long-term agricultural sustainability.

PEST AND DISEASE CONTROL

Pest and disease control is a critical aspect of farming practices to protect crops and ensure optimal yield. Integrated Pest Management (IPM) strategies combine biological, cultural, and chemical methods to control pests while minimizing environmental impact. Biological control involves introducing natural predators to regulate pest populations, while cultural practices, such as crop rotation and companion planting, disrupt the life cycle of pests. Judicious use of pesticides is necessary, with an emphasis on environmentally friendly and targeted applications to avoid unintended consequences.

Regular monitoring of crops for signs of pests and diseases allows farmers to implement timely and effective control measures.

HARVESTING AND POST-HARVEST HANDLING

Harvesting marks the culmination of the farming cycle, and proper techniques are essential to preserve crop quality. The timing of harvest depends on the crop's maturity and intended use. Mechanical harvesting is common for large-scale operations, while hand harvesting may be preferred for delicate or specialty crops. Post-harvest handling involves activities such as cleaning, sorting, and packaging to maintain product quality. Cold storage facilities and transportation infrastructure play a crucial role in preserving perishable crops. Additionally, value-added processing, such as canning or drying, extends the shelf life of harvested products and enhances marketability. Efficient post-harvest practices are vital to minimize losses and ensure a reliable food supply chain.

CHAPTER FIVE

TOOLS AND TECHNOLOGY

CRUCIAL FARM TOOLS

Essential farm equipment is crucial to guaranteeing effective and productive farming methods in modern agriculture. These are essential equipment for many jobs, from harvesting to soil preparation. Perhaps the most important piece of equipment is a tractor, which can be used for planting, cultivating, and plowing, among other tasks. Tractors are equipped with tools like plows, harrows, and seeders to make these jobs easier. Furthermore, by effectively cutting, threshing, and separating grains, combined harvesters have transformed the harvesting process by simplifying a labor-intensive process.

Irrigation systems are another crucial piece of farm equipment that is needed to consistently supply crops with water. Modern irrigation techniques that promote water conservation and maximize crop development include pivot systems, drip irrigation, and sprinkler systems. Tools like cultivators and cultivator shovels aid in controlling weeds, protecting crops, and increasing yields. Silos and barns, among other storage structures, are crucial for maintaining harvested crops and shielding them from the elements.

TECHNOLOGY APPLICATION IN ONION FARMING

Onion farming has been greatly impacted by technology, which has raised crop quality overall and improved efficiency and precision. With the aid of GPS technology and satellite imagery, precision farming techniques enable farmers to assess the unique requirements of their crops. This makes it possible to apply pesticides and fertilizers precisely, cutting down on waste and lessening the impact on the environment. Farmers can now make well-informed judgments on the best ways to cultivate onions thanks to real-time data on crop conditions, soil health, and moisture levels provided by sophisticated monitoring systems, which include sensors and drones.

Technology has also been crucial to the breeding and selection of seeds in the onion industry. greater disease resistance, increased yields, and greater quality onion cultivars have been developed thanks to genetic engineering and marker-assisted breeding. In addition to helping farmers, this also guarantees a steady and abundant supply of onions, which enhances global food security.

EFFICIENCY AND AUTOMATION

A new era of efficiency in agriculture has been brought about by automation, especially in operations that were formerly labor-intensive. Automation is visible at many points during the growing process in the onion industry. Planting has become faster and more consistent because of the replacement of hand seeding with automated planters and seeders. The advent of mechanized harvesting equipment has brought about a shift in the work of harvesting, which previously required a large amount of human effort.

Onion sorting and grading are further expedited by automated systems that categorize onions according to size, shape, and quality using computer vision and machine learning algorithms. This increases the produce's market value while also lightening the farmers' workload. Automated irrigation systems also help conserve water by providing the exact amount of water needed for the best crop growth, guided by sensors and meteorological data.

Enhanced productivity, resource efficiency, and crop quality have resulted from the incorporation of technology and key farm equipment in onion farming. These developments highlight how crucial it is to adopt technical improvements to satisfy the increasing needs of a fast-changing agricultural environment.

CHAPTER SIX

ADVERTISING TECHNIQUES

PACKAGING AND BRANDING

Creating a name or logo is not the only thing that goes into branding, which is an important aspect of marketing. It includes the general impression and sentimental bond that customers have with a brand or business.

Establishing a distinctive value proposition, comprehending the target market, and reliably fulfilling the brand promise are all necessary components of a successful brand strategy. In this process, packaging is important since it is a physical manifestation of the brand.

In addition to safeguarding the goods, good packaging influences consumer decisions by clearly communicating the brand's identity, values, and point of differentiation on the store shelf.

DISTRIBUTION CHANNELS

These are the routes via which goods or services are delivered to customers. To effectively reach target markets, the correct distribution channels must be chosen. This entails taking into account elements including the product's characteristics, the intended market, and current market trends. Businesses have two options for distribution: they can use indirect channels like distributors, wholesalers, and retailers, or they can use direct channels like their own stores or websites. Online channels have also been made possible by the digital age, giving businesses the chance to use e-commerce platforms to connect with customers around the world.

DEVELOPING STRONG TIES WITH BUYERS

Effective marketing is based on developing strong ties with buyers. This entails building trust and loyalty, knowing the requirements and preferences of the consumer, and providing individualized experiences. Tools for customer relationship management (CRM) are essential for gathering and evaluating consumer data so that marketing campaigns can be customized. In addition to financial transactions, customer service, email marketing, and social media interaction all contribute to the development of long-lasting connections. Companies that put a high priority on customer satisfaction and proactively solicit feedback stand to gain from positive word-of-mouth marketing as well as client retention.

STRATEGIES FOR PRICING

Pricing is a crucial component of marketing that has an immediate impact on market competitiveness and consumer perception. When setting prices, businesses need to take into account several factors, including perceived value, competition, and manufacturing costs.

Value-based pricing, cost-plus pricing, and dynamic pricing are some of the strategies. Bundling and other forms of promotional pricing, such as discounts, can also be successful in boosting sales.

Furthermore, psychological pricing strategies might affect customer behavior. One example of this is placing prices slightly below round numbers. To respond to shifting market conditions, pricing plans must be reviewed and modified regularly.

INTERNET PRESENCE AND MARKETING

Due to the changes brought about by the digital era, marketing has become completely dependent on online presence and methods. Search engine optimization (SEO), social media marketing, email campaigns, and content marketing are just a few of the many strategies that make up online marketing. In addition to raising brand awareness, a robust web presence enables businesses to interact instantly with their target market. Businesses can now offer things directly to customers beyond geographical boundaries thanks to e-commerce platforms. Using analytics tools enables marketers to monitor and assess online performance, which enables ongoing strategy optimization to maintain an advantage in the cutthroat digital market.

CHAPTER SEVEN

REGULATORY AND LEGAL ASPECTS

PERMITS AND LICENSES

When it comes to legal and regulatory matters, getting the licenses and permits that a business needs is essential, especially if it operates in an industry like agriculture where restrictions are more stringent. Government authorities issue licenses and permits to firms so they can legally engage in particular activities. Permits for pesticide application, water rights, land use, and other things may fall under this category in the agriculture industry. Obtaining these licenses is crucial for maintaining agricultural operations sustainably and ethically as well as for legal compliance.

Getting licenses and permissions requires negotiating a complicated regulatory landscape that varies depending on the jurisdiction. For agriculture firms to obtain the necessary licenses, they must be knowledgeable about local, state, and federal rules. If licensing standards are not met, there may be fines, legal repercussions, or even an operating suspension. Thus, companies in the agriculture industry must pay close attention to detail and take the initiative to be informed about any changes in regulations.

OBSERVANCE OF AGRICULTURAL STANDARDS

Agricultural standards are essential for maintaining fair trade practices and guaranteeing the quality and safety of agricultural products. Aside from being required by law, adhering to these standards is a way to increase consumer confidence and tap into new markets. Agricultural standards include a broad range of topics, such as labeling procedures, animal welfare, soil management, and pesticide use.

To successfully traverse the agricultural standards landscape, businesses need to be aware of and attentive to the particular rules that apply to their activities. This could entail using sustainable farming methods, following regulations on the use of genetically modified organisms (GMOs), and making sure that goods are properly labeled. Compliance may be checked regularly through audits and inspections, and non-compliance can have serious repercussions including product recalls and reputational harm.

RULES REGARDING THE ENVIRONMENT

The pressure placed on businesses, especially those in the agriculture sector, to comply with strict environmental standards is increasing in tandem with the growing global awareness of environmental issues. The purpose of environmental laws is to lessen the negative effects that agriculture has on ecosystems, water supplies, and air quality. To minimize the ecological footprint, compliance frequently entails controlling waste, cutting pollutants, and implementing sustainable farming techniques.

Navigating environmental rules for agricultural enterprises necessitates a comprehensive strategy that takes the entire supply chain into account. This could entail putting in place erosion control techniques, using water wisely, and embracing technology that reduces greenhouse gas emissions. Environmental regulations must be followed; breaking them may result in fines, harm to one's reputation, or even the need to shut down operations. As a result, in today's environmentally concerned world, integrating ecologically friendly techniques into the foundation of agricultural operations is not only required by law but also highly strategic.

www.ingramcontent.com/pod-product-compliance
Lightning Source LLC
Chambersburg PA
CBHW070844290526
45795CB00002B/983